This book belongs to

· · · · · · · · · · · ·

NOAH and his Ark

First published in Great Britain in 2017

Society for Promoting Christian Knowledge
36 Causton Street, London SW1P 4ST
www.spck.org.uk

Text copyright © Alexa Tewkesbury 2017
Illustrations copyright © Dani Padrón 2017

British Library Cataloguing-in-Publication Data
A catalogue record for this book is available from the British Library

ISBN 978-0-281-07496-9

Typeset by Gill McLean
Printed in Great Britain by Ashford Colour Press

1 3 5 7 9 10 8 6 4 2

Produced on paper from sustainable forests

NOAH and his Ark

Alexa Tewkesbury

Illustrated by Dani Padrón

SPCK

Bang! thumps the hammer. **Bang-bong** . . . .
Zoop! hacks the saw. **Zoop-shoop.**

I'm building an ark with my three strong sons.
I'm building a great ark because God has asked me to.

In go the creatures, into the ark. 'Load them up,' God says, 'two of every kind from all across the world.'

'Now, **where** have those spiders got to?'

'Squawk!' screech the birds. 'Squawk-quark.'
'Oink!' grunt the pigs. 'Oink-oink.'

This is taking a very long time.
The animals are **sooo** noisy.
I hope they don't give Mrs Noah a headache!

Shuffle, trundle the tortoises. **Shuffle-scuff** . . .
Creak, groans the ark.
Creak-squeak.

All aboard,
so we can get that door closed!
I do hope there'll be enough
room for me.

'You're just in time,'
says Mrs Noah.
'Look at that purple sky.
Here comes the rain.'

Splish,
splashes the rain.
Splish-splosh.
Up comes the flood,
up and up.

We're snug in here, my family and all the animals. I'm glad God asked me to build a boat.

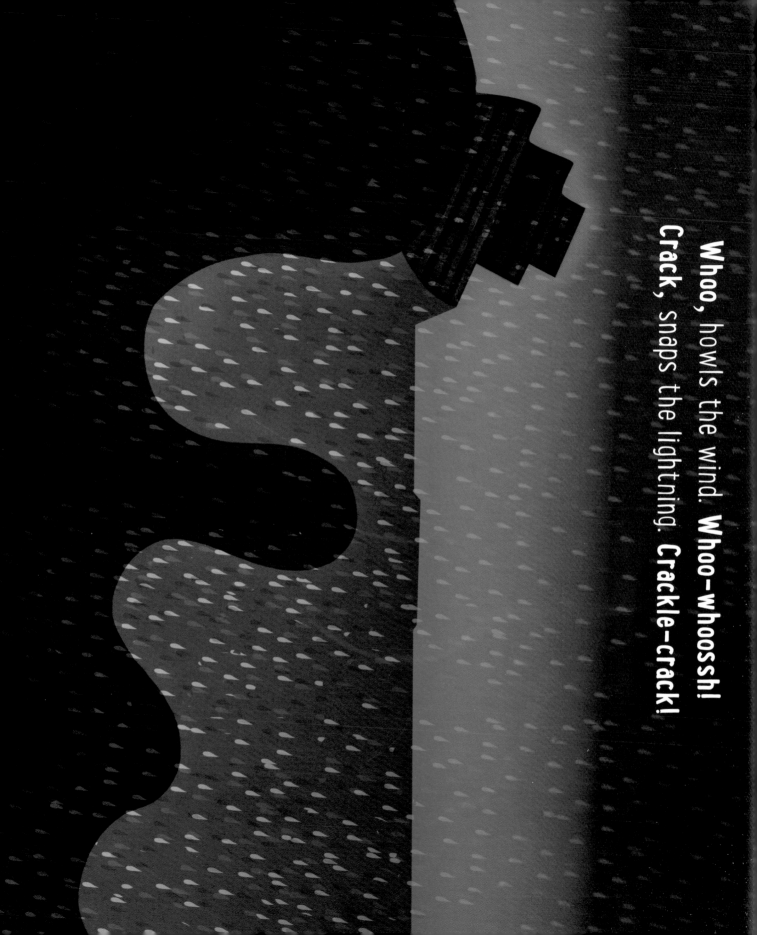

Whoo, howls the wind. Whoo–whooosh!
Crack, snaps the lightning. Crackle–crack!

Our boat is afloat! We ride the storm-jumbled water.

Day after night, night after day, rising, falling on the jumbly waves.

Until, one day,
Mrs Noah looks up.

'Well, I never.
It's stopping.
I do believe
the rain is stopping.'

Stopping??

'Off you fly, raven.
Look for some dry land,' says Noah.

'Your turn, little dove.
I wish I could fly.
I fancy getting off this ark.'

'Nothing? Ah, well . . .'

'Coo,' croons the dove. 'Vroo-coo.'
'Hooray!' we all cheer. 'Hooray-hoorah!'

The dove holds a twig.
A twig from an olive tree that has
its roots in good, firm ground.

God is drying out the earth at last.

Ssh. Quiet now, **ssh-ssh** . . .
Hush. Listen out, **hush-shush.**

Can you hear it? All around. God's peace.
God has washed the world clean with his rain.

Thank you, God.

'Chortle,' chuckle the animals. 'Chortle-snort.'
Flutter, flit the butterflies. Flutter-flick.

'Here's my rainbow,' God says.

'A sign of my promise: there will never be so much rain on the earth again.'

No wonder the animals chuckle.
I'm chuckling, too.
God kept us safe
through the great flood.
I always knew he would.

Can you spot . . . .

① Butterflies

② Parrots

③ Foxes

④ Hedgehogs

⑤ Cats

⑧ Storks

⑫ Ladybirds

⑦ Dove

⑪ Birds

⑥ Raven

⑩ Spiders

⑨ Toucans

Other titles in the series
by Alexa Tewkesbury

Jonah and the Whale
978-0-281-07500-3

Daniel in the Lions' Den
978-0-281-07498-3

SPCK
www.spck.org.uk